Real People

Christopher Reeve

By Philip Abraham

Welcome
Books

Children's Press®
A Division of Scholastic Inc.
New York / Toronto / London / Auckland / Sydney
Mexico City / New Delhi / Hong Kong
Danbury, Connecticut

Photo Credits: Cover, pp. 5, 11, 15, 19, 21 © AP/Wide World Photos;
p. 7 © Lynn Goldsmith/CORBIS; p. 9 © M. Ferguson/The Gamma Liaison Network;
p. 13 © Mitchell Gerber/CORBIS; p. 17 © Reuters NewMedia Inc./CORBIS

Contributing Editor: Jennifer Silate
Book Design: Christopher Logan

Library of Congress Cataloging-in-Publication Data

Abraham, Philip, 1970–
 Christopher Reeve / by Philip Abraham
  p. cm. — (Real people)
 Includes index.
Summary: This is an easy-to-read biography of the actor Christopher Reeve,
noting the accident that left him paralyzed.
 ISBN 0-516-23951-1 (lib. bdg.) — ISBN 0-516-23602-4 (pbk.)
 1. Reeve, Christopher, 1952– —Juvenile literature. 2. Actors—United States—
Biography—Juvenile literature. 3. Quadriplegics—United States—Biography—
Juvenile literature. [1. Reeve, Christopher, 1952– 2. Actors and actresses.
3. Quadriplegics. 4. Physically handicapped.] I. Title. II. Series.

PN2287.R292 A24 2002
791.43'028'092—dc21

          00-043184
2001042358

Contents

1 Acting 4

2 Horseback Riding 10

3 The Accident 12

4 New Words 22

5 To Find Out More 23

6 Index 24

7 About the Author 24

Meet Christopher Reeve.

He is an **actor**.

Christopher is a very good actor.

He has been in many movies and plays.

Christopher played Superman in the movies.

That **role** made him **famous**.

9

Christopher also liked to ride horses.

In 1995, Christopher was in a horseback riding **accident**.

Now, Christopher has to use a **wheelchair**.

13

He cannot move his arms or legs.

Christopher's wife, Dana, has helped him a lot since his accident.

Christopher still works on movies.

He works very hard.